INTRODUCTION

This book is designed for adults
to read with children.

Opportunities are there to share your
thoughts about life and nature.

Today, we will be meeting
Dandelions
with
Cassie

Meeting Wildflowers

Growing Wild and Free in America
Just Like You and Me

By Kathryn Felton

Meeting Wildflowers
Growing Wild and Free in America
Just like You and Me

ISBN: 978-1-964462-84-4 (sc)
ISBN: 978-1-964462-85-1 (e)

Rev. date: 11/07/2024

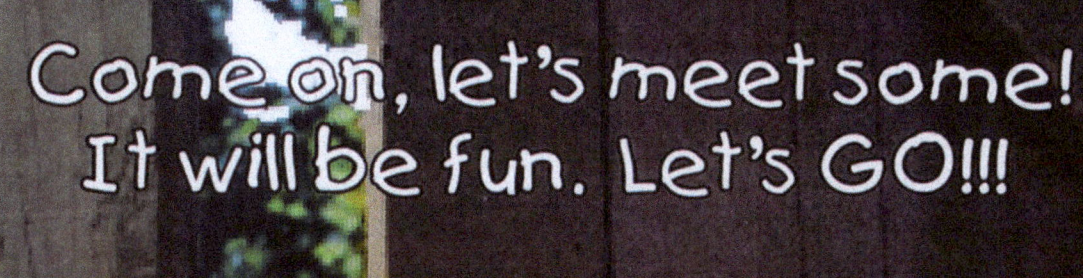

Come on, let's meet some!
It will be fun. Let's GO!!!

Freshen up,
my lady.
She's going to
introduce us.

You will like them, I know
you will.
Visiting flowers and stuff
can be a thrill.

We are
Thrillin'!!!

In the spring, I look carefully around in the grass

The I took a little spin around.
Of course it's not too fast.

Hey Baby!!!
Easy on the
footwork.

12

Aha! I knew it!
Here they are...
All over the ground.

Now, to let
their beauty
sink in,
I need to sit
right down.

13

See this one?
Isn't it cute?

I pulled it
up from the root.

Thank you root
for keeping me
alive! You bring
me water and
nutrients from
the soil so I can
survive!

Take it
easy!

14

15

They look like this when they grow older.

I think, Gray becomes Us......

16

They make more seeds
and start all over!!

We are cycle NATURALLY.

They grow from seeds into pretty flowers.

You can look at them and play with them for hours and hours

Now Dandelions
are wild flowers,
and I like them.
Do you? I hope you
can find a bunch
of them too.

Some people think
that they're just
a bunch of weeds!
But, in a tea, they
provide for many
of our needs.

That's my Story.
It's been fun!
Later I'll tell you another one.

WOW! Wonder who we'll meet next...

Now wildflowers are our friends.
Let me explain about them again.

When you mix us
All together.

We live in peace,
And blend forever.

For we are all different
Colors and kinds.

But, blended together
The BEAUTY
Will blow your mind.

Meeting Autumn Wildflowers
with
Logan and Annie

Goldenrods and Asters, their beauty will explode.
For Autumn is a miracle of Lavender and Gold.

OK! Autumn is here and I
am heading out...To see
the wild flowers that are
starting to SPROUT!

Now, I'm just starting out,
so have no fear..
I can assure you that way
more than this Morning
Glory are here.

Oh yes, that's my girlfriend
over there!
Isn't she sweet?
She thinks,
the Purple Asters are ever so neat

And, these Purple Cosmos...
They are actually quite delicate and mild.

They make me think of you and your
adorable little smile

Oh, there you are! Enjoying more up on the hill.
I see you still love purple. Come over here and
check out this thrill.

Russian Sage

Whoa!!! How about these Cosmos down by the river?
And these by the yard will surely
make her heart quiver

I know, let's get together, and work very hard,
and plant some nature of our own
RIGHT HERE in the yard.

Then, we will have beautiful nature to inspire us
for the rest of our life.
And maybe, maybe, one day,
you can even be my Wife!!!

Meeting Summer Wildflowers with
Zack, Katie, Dani, Nick, Courtney, and Jordan

Poppies, Bachelor Buttons

33

Well it is summer, and I can take a moment here to think. My creating mind and imagination will startle the future before I can blink.

"June is busting out all over,
The feeling is getting so intense."

35

Speaking of intense, these wild flowers
are quite pleasant and inspiring.
They just grow wild and pretty everywhere.
What good stuff are you conspiring?

Speaking of intense... I must stop and ponder my future too.
There are so many amazing things to do.
After all, I'm headed for manhood
and soon I must choose.
How will I decide? I'll wait for some clues.

And Girls will be inspired
out in nature too.
I wonder what ideas will
come to you.

It is even more amazing what we can be,
When we can grow up in our land that is free.

And don't worry,
there will be peace one of these days.
Life won't always be in such a haze.

Good times will come and good times will go,
but they will be back again, before you know.

And, we know that everyone wants to have fun. Well we can, and still Share a little Love, with everyone.

Just pause
in the silence...
With nature
all around...
And the new
thoughts
and ideas
that come to you
will be profound.

Follow up advice and insights from Twins Nathan and Mabry

Please do not take this beauty
around you for granted.
Protect it, defend it, or we'll all be empty-handed.

Now, Nature gives us beauty and can cure many things. But, we MUST be careful, because some stuff might cause PAIN. So, please obey the rules, because some rules just need to be. Then you can enjoy our Earth, FREE and NATURALLY.

But do be careful when you wonder free.
Yes, do take care.
Sometimes dangers may be lurking out there.
Wildlife is beautiful, but be careful what you pick.
It is no fun getting injured from
a splinter, thorn, or tick!

And take lots of time to laugh and smile and giggle and grin. Because many doctors do agree that laughter makes your body win. It helps your heart, your breathing, and your ever-growing mind. It helps your blood fight the germs and keeps you healthy all the time.

"Laughter is the best medicine"
(Dr. William Fry, Stanford University)

Remember the old hymn:
For the beauty of the earth,
for the beauty of the skies
for the love which from our birth
Over and around us lies.
Lord of all to thee we raise
This, our hymn of grateful praise.

By, Folliot S. Pierpoint (1835-1917)

And when you need advice:

According to a man of ancient days, Asher Ben Ammi, who walked with Jesus over 2000 years ago: "You may find Him anywhere, and everywhere, for truly He lives within your heart. Go within the silence as He has taught you, and find Him there...He waits for you even now."
From Ronald Way's "Ancient Memories"